D1384514

INTO Wild Louisiana

BLACKBIRCH®
PRESS

THOMSON

™

GALE

San Diego • Detroit • New York • San Francisco • Cleveland • New Haven, Conn. • Waterville, Maine • London • Munich

THOMSON

GALE

For more information, contact
The Gale Group, Inc.
27500 Drake Rd.
Farmington Hills, MI 48331-3535
Or you can visit our Internet site at http://www.gale.com

LIBRARY OF CONGRESS CATALOGING-IN-PUBLICATION DATA

Into wild Louisiana / Elaine Pascoe, book editor.
    p. cm. — (The Jeff Corwin experience)
Summary: Television personality Jeff Corwin takes the reader on an expedition through the bayous of Louisiana, and introduces some of the diverse wildife found there.
Includes bibliographical references and index.
    ISBN 1-4103-0060-9 (hardback : alk. paper) — ISBN 1-4103-0181-8 (pbk. : alk. paper)
    1. Zoology—Louisiana—Juvenile literature. [1. Zoology—Louisiana. 2. Louisiana—Description and travel. 3. Corwin, Jeff.] I. Pascoe, Elaine. II. Corwin, Jeff. III. Series.

QL179.I58 2004
591.9763—dc21   2003009277

Printed in China
10 9 8 7 6 5 4 3 2 1

E ver since I was a kid, I dreamed about traveling around the world, visiting exotic places, and seeing all kinds of incredible animals. And now, guess what? That's exactly what I get to do!

Yes, I am incredibly lucky. But, you don't have to have your own television show on Animal Planet to go off and explore the natural world around you. I mean, I travel to Madagascar and the Amazon and all kinds of really cool places—but I don't need to go that far to see amazing wildlife up close. In fact, I can find thousands of incredible critters right here, in my own backyard—or in my neighbor's yard (he does get kind of upset when he finds me crawling around in the bushes, though). The point is, no matter where you are, there's fantastic stuff to see in nature. All you have to do is look.

I love snakes, for example. Now, I've come face to face with the world's most venomous vipers—some of the biggest, some of the strongest, and some of the rarest. But I've also found an amazing variety of snakes just traveling around my home state of Massachusetts. And I've taken trips to preserves, and state parks, and national parks—and in each place I've enjoyed unique and exciting plants and animals. So, if I can do it, you can do it, too (except for the hunting venomous snakes part!). So, plan a nature hike with some friends. Organize some projects with your science teacher at school. Ask mom and dad to put a state or a national park on the list of things to do on your next family vacation. Build a bird house. Whatever. But get out there.

As you read through these pages and look at the photos, you'll probably see how jazzed I get when I come face to face with beautiful animals. That's good. I want you to feel that excitement. And I want you to remember that—even if you don't have your own TV show—you can still experience the awesome beauty of nature almost anywhere you go—any day of the week. I only hope that I can help bring that awesome power and beauty a little closer to you. Enjoy!

Best Wishes!

Jeff

INTO
Wild Louisiana

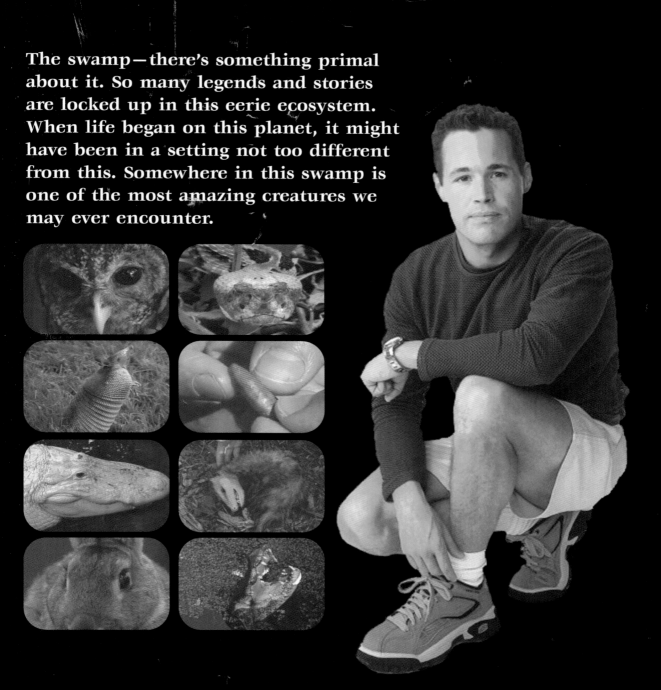

The swamp—there's something primal about it. So many legends and stories are locked up in this eerie ecosystem. When life began on this planet, it might have been in a setting not too different from this. Somewhere in this swamp is one of the most amazing creatures we may ever encounter.

I'm Jeff Corwin.
Welcome to Louisiana.

Louisiana is filled with swamps and bayous.

This is a beautiful barred owl.

The swamps and bayous of Louisiana are home to some extraordinary wildlife, like this beautiful bird of prey. She's a barred owl. These owls are amazing birds, with extraordinary vision. Her big eyes are excellent for spotting prey at night. The price she pays for having such good eyesight and such large eyes is

An incredible mix of creatures lives in the unique habitat.

Look at those huge eyes.

Time to fly.

that she can't individually move her eyeballs. Instead, she rotates her head to spot prey.

I didn't actually capture this animal; she's part of a rehabilitation and release program. She's done her homework, mastered the art of capturing prey, and now she's ready to take on the wilds of the Louisiana swamps once again. Away she goes, on a great adventure.

I love owls. I love Louisiana. Let's get started on our own great adventure.

This massive pile of rubble is part of an old sugarcane mill. Now, sugarcane attracts rats. And rats attract one very special predator— special to me, at least, because I'm a herpetologist. It's the canebrake rattlesnake. Isn't he beautiful? But I need to hold this snake so that he can't strike me because he is very venomous.

Guess what's hanging out at the old sugarcane mill...

This is a type of venomous snake that you don't want to pin with a stick. He's active, pretty spunky, and if I were to pin him there's a good chance that I would injure him. He'd probably pull his head back really fast, and I might injure his spine.

...a beautiful canebrake rattlesnake.

I'd also expose myself to a serious bite. This snake has huge venom glands and very long opposable fangs, and he can inject copious amounts of venom if he chooses. He can deliver a dry bite, but if you get a wet bite you're getting a lot of potent, tissue-destroying venom inside you. There are legends about these animals taking down people and animals. The stories say that, in the old days, plantations lost so many mules to snakebites while hauling cane from the fields that they'd have replacement mules lined up, ready to go.

These guys are very venomous.

Timber and canebrake rattlesnakes are disappearing very quickly from the landscape. In just a matter of years it may take some serious conservation efforts to keep them around. We'll let this guy go find himself a nice rat.

Going deeper into the swamp, the feeling of isolation increases. It's just me and the animals that call this place home. This is frog country.

And this is the green tree frog, a very common amphibian in the ancient cypress trees around these swamps. You can also find these frogs in the gutters of houses or hanging underneath very moist shingles. During the daytime, these animals like to stay where it's nice and moist. That's why this fellow was hiding out in the crevice of a very squishy, rotten log.

The tree frogs are mostly nocturnal, so they come out at night. During

Under this wet, squishy log...

...is a little green tree frog.

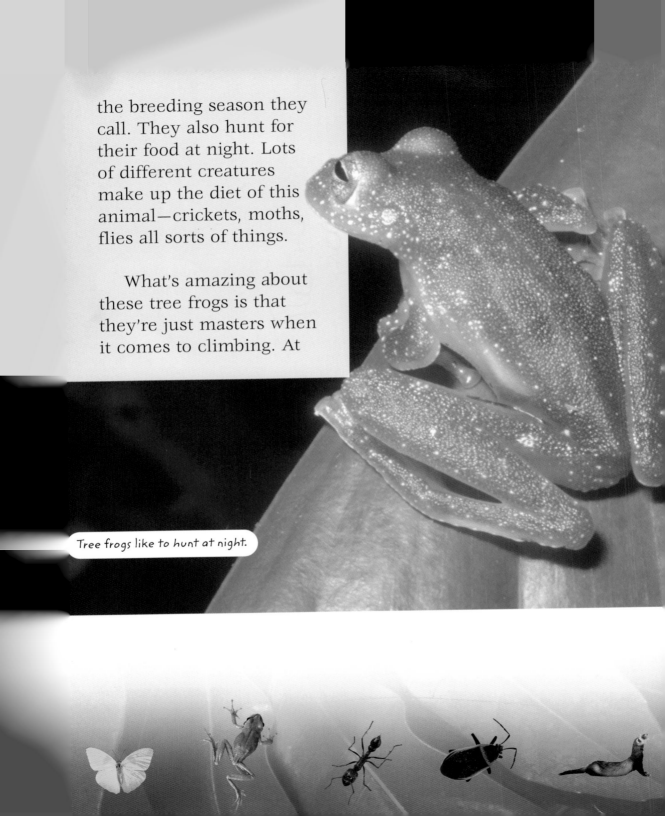

the breeding season they call. They also hunt for their food at night. Lots of different creatures make up the diet of this animal—crickets, moths, flies all sorts of things.

What's amazing about these tree frogs is that they're just masters when it comes to climbing. At

Tree frogs like to hunt at night.

Little suction discs make their feet hold to almost anything.

Putting the little guy back.

the tip of each finger is a suction disc, and that disc creates a vacuum on the surface that the frog is climbing on. The frog can hang upside down. It can adhere to a surface as smooth as glass.

I'm going to place him right back in this little cranny of his rotten tree.

Here's a speckled king snake.

Look at this. If you look at the earth, you'll see there's a coil, and that coil is part of the body of a wonderful, wonderful snake. This is a speckled king snake.

I can hold this snake...

I can handle this snake, let him crawl all over, and he won't strike. Here's the secret: I rely on this animal's primary way of moving in its environment, and that is to slide across the surface of the earth or the surface of tree branches. As long as I can make my hands like those surfaces, he's not threatened. I'm just a part of his ecosystem.

King snakes are called kings because they like to eat other snakes, and it is not impossible for an animal like this to prey on rattlesnakes or other venomous serpents. They're amazing creatures, and beautiful.

These gorgeous creatures will eat other snakes.

Looking for a good swimming hole? Well, you definitely don't want to be swimming in this pond. Underneath this blanket of water hyacinth are about 30,000 or 40,000 pounds of alligators. This beautiful pond is an important breeding site for these animals.

Uh-oh. Trouble coming...

In fact, we've got two adults right here, which I'm going to pass very carefully.

Gator eggs incubate for sixty to seventy days.

When these gators build a nest, whether they know it or not, they're creating a compost heap. All the reeds and grasses stacked together begin to decay, and that decaying process creates heat energy. Thus the compost heap becomes an incubator for the gator eggs. It takes about sixty to seventy days for those eggs to cook up to the point of hatching, and at that point the mother comes back to the nest. What draws her to it is the sound of the baby gators calling from inside the eggs. The mother then picks up each egg and bites the shell to help the baby out.

In my hands I've got a young alligator, probably about three or four years in age. They grow about a foot each year. And this one is just about at that point in its life where he can relax a little bit, because gators any younger than this are wide open to a great array of predators.

The alligator's tail is a tool for propulsion; it's how he maneuvers through the water. Essentially, this animal is designed to hunt. And, of course, the best tools are in his mouth. He has a deadly collection of teeth along the bottom jaw and the top jaw, and when he closes his mouth those teeth overlap. As you can see, some of the teeth actually hang outside of the jaw.

This guy is about three or four years old.

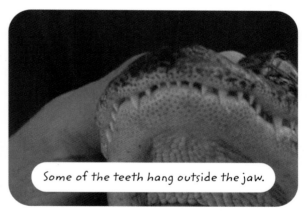

Some of the teeth hang outside the jaw.

The gator's whole body will be underwater while he's hunting — only his eyes will remain on the surface.

When he's hunting, a gator's whole body is submerged, and his eyes just sort of scan the surface looking for his prey. Even the eyes are camouflaged, designed to disappear in the mucky water. Now, if everything goes well with this creature, and he has a chance to avoid becoming dinner for other animals, he might reach 15 or 16 feet in length. It's not common, but there are gators that big swimming around this swamp and through other parts of the South.

Armadillos can't see too well, but they can smell.

We're about 25 to 30 miles outside of New Orleans, at an old military bunker site. What's great about this place is that it's a habitat for a huge population of a very weird mammals native to North, Central, and South America—armadillos. Armadillos don't have very good vision, but they have excellent senses of smell and hearing. They can run pretty fast, too. But as long as we sneak up very quietly, we can get close and even catch one.

This amazing prehistoric-looking animal is a nine-banded armadillo. Armadillos spend most of the daytime hours underground. Then, when the sun starts to set, they emerge and do their foraging. They look for ants, termites, and worms, especially earthworms. They have some extraordinary claws, which are wonderful for ripping the earth apart as they search for food.

These claws are perfect for ripping open ant hills.

The armadillo's number one way of protecting itself is its armor. Its skin is plate-like, as you can see, and in front of the two major plates are smaller plates that telescope, so the animal is almost like an accordion.

Covered in plates.

Aren't the armadillos great? I love them. But just down the road a little ways is the Big Easy, New Orleans, and a chance for us to encounter a creature that you would never see in the wild.

This is an 8-foot American alligator. Anatomically and physically, he's just like every other alligator you'd see out there floating in the bayous, except in one way. Because of one tiny little genetic difference, melanophores—or pigment sites—aren't present on this animal. He's got color around his eyes, and he's not a true albino. But most of his body is pink or whitish in color—and most amazing, he has blue eyes. This is the first time I've ever seen an alligator with blue eyes.

This color for a gator is very rare.

Now, here's a great question: Why would you not see an animal this big in the wild with this sort of color? Two major reasons. Reason number one is that when this creature hatches out, and it's about 6 to 8 inches in length, its light color is a lure for predators. It doesn't have natural camouflage. It sticks out, and it's an easy target. Reason number two is that, as a predator, it's visible. It's obvious to the prey it's trying to hunt, so it's not going to be very successful. Those are probably the two greatest reasons why an alligator like this is such a rare sight, especially in a wild situation.

OK, back to the swamp. Let's go see what other creatures are lurking in this watery wilderness.

The flood waters of as many as thirty-eight states find their way to the Atchafalaya Basin, which covers more than 70 miles of south-central Louisiana. This liquid habitat is a continually changing maze of bayous, streams, and lakes, and is home to a diverse array of creatures.

Lots of water here in Louisiana.

Here's a cottonmouth.

This is one of the creatures I really like a lot. It's an animal that has served as a seed for many of the legends that weave their way throughout this swamp. It's the infamous cottonmouth, or water moccasin.

The white inside the mouth is how this guy got his name.

These snakes have two opposable fangs.

Look at that leathery skin.

I caught this snake fairly easily because he's getting ready to shed. I can tell he's going to shed because his eyes and his skin are blue. He's in what's called the opaque cycle. I'm holding him very gently, and clearly if you ever encounter a water moccasin you'd never do this.

Look inside his mouth. He's got a pair of opposable fangs, and he uses those fangs both as a tool to grab onto the prey and to inject the prey or predator with venom. And that mouth is white, white, white. Cottonmouth.

This is a Tabasco pepper tree.

This is a pepper tree, specifically a Tabasco pepper tree, and these are the individual peppers. As they turn reddish orange, they're ripe. This is when they're at their hottest stage. Louisiana is well known for its culture, its folklore, its history, its amazing wildlife, and its spice. Tabasco sauce is a staple on just about every table in Louisiana and every cupboard throughout North America.

When they turn reddish, they're ready.

Some Tabasco sauce in the making...yum.

Tabasco is made by an ancient method. Peppers are ground up into a sauce and then placed in wooden barrels to age for about three years. A lot of craftsmanship goes into the process, and one of the most interesting steps is making these barrels.

Ground up peppers are aged in barrels.

We got Hamilton, one of the craftsmen who specializes in making the barrels, to demonstrate how it's done. Then we asked him to point us in the direction of one of Louisiana's neatest animals—the black bear.

Here's Hamilton—he makes the barrels.

Steve Reagan and Janet Ertel are wildlife biologists who are doing an amazing study on black bears through the U.S. Fish and Wildlife Service. They can get us up close and personal with a Louisiana black bear.

I know they look cute, but these are poweful animlas.

These are my friends Steve and Janet.

This is _not_ how a bear sleeps.

A dart is shot through a blow pipe to calm the animal.

We followed a signal from a bear that Steve and Janet previously tagged, and it led us to this culvert trap. The bear is inside. She's sleeping— but even so, Janet warns me not to touch the culvert because the could wake up su and lash out with claws. The biolog blow dart to sedate the bear, and we and sedative to kick in.

If she's covered, she'll stay calm.

Look at those amazing claws.

Then we remove the dart, cover her face so she'll have no stimulation, and start gathering information—temperature and other data—in the least invasive way possible. You can get a good look at the animal's claws, strong enough to shimmy up a tree, rip open a nest, and to take down prey, but delicate enough to tweeze berries off bushes. Notice her amazing lips, which she can manipulate to open jars. What you can't see is her smell. She smells like dried milk.

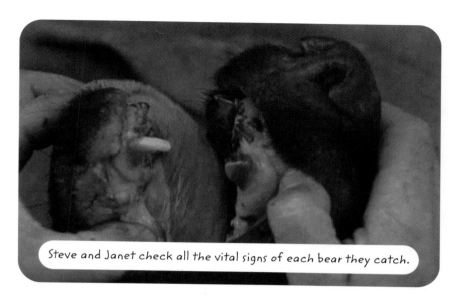

Steve and Janet check all the vital signs of each bear they catch.

Her temperature is normal for a bear—between 98 and 100 degrees. The wear on her teeth shows that she's old, probably about 15 years old. We take measurements and a sample of hair for genetic and chemical studies, and then hoist her up to get her weight, 150 pounds. In about an hour our bear is starting to wake up.

This bear weighed 150 pounds.

This looks sad...

This is so sad. Don't die, little buddy. Come back.

Actually, this animal isn't dead. This is an amazing thing, one of nature's greatest survival strategies. It's called playing possum or playing dead or feigning death. The opossum lies here, producing some nasty smells at the back end. He's got a little phlegm leaking out of his mouth.

...but it's an opossum...playing possum.

Opossums are nocturnal marsupials.

33

Although he's packed with protein, to a predator he comes across as an animal that probably would not make the best meal.

What makes opossums unique? Well, they're

marsupials. Other marsupials include kangaroos, wallabies, and wombats; but opossums are North America's only true marsupial. And what's special about marsupials is the way they reproduce. Just like all mammals, they give birth to live offspring. But when this creature's babies are born, they're smaller than your fingernail.

This guy is well equipped to hunt— look at those claws.

A female opossum can give birth to ten, maybe even a dozen babies. And you can fit a whole brood of baby opossums in a tablespoon at birth—that's how small they are. They immediately climb into the mother's pouch, where they nurse for the next couple of months.

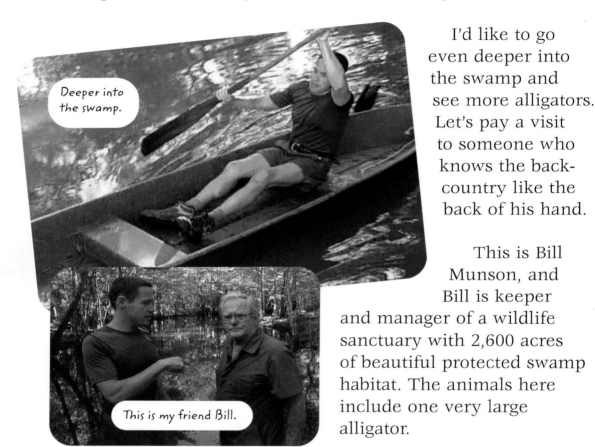

Deeper into the swamp.

This is my friend Bill.

I'd like to go even deeper into the swamp and see more alligators. Let's pay a visit to someone who knows the back-country like the back of his hand.

This is Bill Munson, and Bill is keeper and manager of a wildlife sanctuary with 2,600 acres of beautiful protected swamp habitat. The animals here include one very large alligator.

Look at the size of this guy. His head is about a foot and a half in length from the tip of its snout to the back of its eyes. He's about 15 feet in length and probably weighs a good 1,500 pounds. He's probably over one hundred years

This guy is probably one hundred years old.

old. A colossal creature, and he's nearly invisible. You could be walking along these banks and never know this alligator was there.

There's a huge gator in there somewhere.

Look at that camouflage.

Bill has lured this giant to us by feeding him a few pieces of chicken. Feeding these wild animals is controversial. There's concern that handing out food could get them used to people, and then they could become dangerous. But Bill says the amount he feeds is just a small part of the animal's daily diet, and the handouts serve a good purpose—they keep the gator coming in for checkups. Also, this wild swamp is closed to fishing and hunting, so there are not many people around.

Here...gator, gator.

The guy likes chicken.

Of course, if this gator were to latch onto my arm, I'd very quickly be part of the food chain.

Moving all around me are about a thousand creatures. If you don't like mosquitoes—and I don't—you do not want to spend summertime in the swamps of Louisiana. But there is one creature here that is precious. It's the swamp rabbit.

Now, normally this would be a tough animal for us to see. Swamp rabbits are very common, by no means endangered or rare creatures, but they're elusive. They've

Here's a swamp rabbit.

You don't see these rabbits much.

got excellent camouflage for blending in with their habitat, and they have some unique behaviors that allow them to avoid becoming prey.

This individual is part of a rehab program. He was found as a baby rabbit, and now he's ready to be released.

That gives us a chance to experience what makes him so special. This rabbit can do something that you've probably never seen a rabbit do before, and that's swim. Swim like Esther Williams.

These guys are common in Louisiana, but they're hard to spot.

I might disappear into the mud....

Got him! This is one big alligator snapping turtle.

This mud will swallow you if you let it. We're in the Tchefuncte river system, and there is a reason why I've selected this particular spot. Living right in this area is the largest alligator snapping turtle you are ever going to see. It's an individual that's being used in a breeding program for these animals.

The alligator snapping turtle is the largest species of freshwater turtle in the Americas, and it's probably one of the top two or three freshwater turtles you're going to find in the entire world. Looking at this animal just blows you away—you feel like you've stepped back in time millions of years. This is an animal that has gone from one generation to the next, right on through the age of the dinosaurs into contemporary time periods, with very little change to its design.

This creature looks like he comes from the age of the dinosaurs.

An alligator snapping turtle captures prey just by staying still and allowing himself to disappear. He lies at the bottom of a pond or river, and he just sits there with his mouth open, agape, and lets the prey come to him. If you look

Look at this prehistoric-looking creature.

Inside the mouth is a fleshy lure.

inside this creature's mouth, around the tongue region, you'll discover a small, fleshy structure. It's a lure, and as the turtle sits there with his mouth open, he twitches and dangles that lure. He's waiting for some stupid fish to swim by. Sure enough, a fish comes along and sees what looks like a little salamander. That fish thinks he's going to have dinner, but—bam! He is dinner.

See you next time!

People that live in this area grew up hunting these turtles, but most don't hunt turtles anymore. That's simply because these animals are disappearing— because of over- hunting, loss of habitat, and other factors. And there's a good chance, a very tragic chance, that in the next five or ten years this animal will be endangered. It would be a tremendous loss to American natural history if a fantastic beast such as the alligator snapping turtle should disappear.

Now, this is what Louisiana's all about—amazing creatures like this turtle. Our experience here was great. It was exciting to maneuver up those bayous and see all that wonderful wildlife. I'll see you again on our next wildlife adventure.

Glossary

amphibian a cold-blooded, aquatic animal such as a frog
bayous marshy, sluggish creeks from rivers or inlets from the Gulf of Mexico
compost decaying organic matter such as leaves and other vegetation
conservation preservation or protection
copious a large amount
ecosystem a community of organisms
endangered a species whose population is so low it may become extinct
foraging wandering and searching for food on the ground
habitat a place where animals and plants live naturally together
herpetologist a scientist who studies reptiles
marsupials mammals that carry their young in a pouch, such as kangaroos
    or opossums
melanophores cells that contain melanin, or pigment
nocturnal animals that sleep in the daytime and hunt or forage at night
playing possum pretending to be dead
predator an animal that kills and eat other animals
propulsion forward movement
rehabilitation healing and restoring strength
sanctuary a place where animals are safe and protected
sedative a drug that calms or puts an animal to sleep
serpents snakes
swamp a wetland with much woody vegetation
venom a poison used by snakes to attack their prey or defend themselves
venomous having a gland that produces poison for self-defense or hunting

Index